Province of

Quebec

A vitaminized supplement to classic tourist guides.

Cristina & Olivier Rebière

TABLE OF CONTENTS

Thank you for purchasing this eBook and welcome to your guide *Voyage Experience*: **"Province of Quebec"** which, we hope, will help you discover a part of this great country: magnificent landscapes, dynamic cities, mountains, lakes and an extraordinary nature.

This paper book is made after an ebook that you can have for free on your smartphone or Kindle (see at the end of the book the modalities) and where you can use all the features explained in the following section: "How to use this eguide", and also contains fully functional navigation modes called GeoNav, PhotoNav and IcoNav. The eGuide offers another approach to travel, between "road book" and classic guide. You can imagine that we do not have a team like the *Lonely Planet*, so you will not find in this e-book full of addresses of accommodation or restaurants. We share with you our travels, our experiences. We hope this will help you discover new destinations and make you want to visit them. Note that the electronic version works almost like a website and does not need to be used with an internet connection (unless you want to access "*OpenStreetMap*" and other hyperlinks that we give you throughout the book). We apologize if you find any minor spelling or grammar mistakes in the text. We are self-published authors and despite our frequent re-readings, it may happen that some typos escape us. Thank you for your patience and understanding!

Bon voyage!

Sincerely,

Cristina & Olivier

Practical tips for Canada

Formalities

There is no need for a visa for French or European nationals. An international driving license is strongly recommended if you rent a car and don't want to have any problems.

Budget Tips

Depending on your country of origin, the tips can be different to have cheaper flight tickets. Here are some advices which may apply, no matter where you are coming from.

Buy your tickets in advance (minimum 3 months) to benefit from the best rates; if you have the possibility to choose the dates of your holidays, prefer those where there are promotions on the different airlines. Do not buy your tickets right away, but "test" the market first. Look for the airlines that serve Canada first. See here for the companies that arrive at the Quebec City Airport http://www.aeroportdequebec.com/en and here for Montreal https://www.admtl.com/en/volines/air-companies

Pay attention because the tickets prices may vary on every hour and without any logic. Consequently, record in a file on your computer the prices you have found for several days before making your decision. This way, you can track, compare and know immediately when you will have an opportunity not to be missed. You can save more than 300 €/ticket and even more in certain cases. If possible, avoid traveling at holiday times (Christmas, New Year, etc.) to get the cheapest price for your airline tickets. The National Holiday is the 1st of July for all Canada. However, Quebec's inhabitants attach more importance to St John the Baptist's day, the 24th of June. Depending on your starting point, try the following airlines to have more chances to get good prices: Air Canada, American Airlines, Air Transat, Corsair, KLM, Lufthansa, Emirates.

If you do not like the cold, plan your trip in summer - July and August, but beware that Canadians have also their school holidays. You could hardly find housing availability, unless you book enough time in advance. If you do not fear the cold, I recommend the months of September or October since nature is beautifully colored - the famous "Indian summer". Another charming period lasts from April to June. In May, June and September you can have temperatures going up to 20°C, but also down to 9°C.

Travelling

Renting a car is the best way of getting around if you want to visit Quebec and its surroundings. If you want to visit only the city of Quebec, then you can do it without problems on foot.

Pay attention: it is necessary to guarantee the car rental with a credit card. Make your reservation on the Internet because the price difference is big, even double if you take the vehicle at the airport without prior reservation. We rented a car for 22 days for 965 € here https://www.rentalcars.com/en/ insurance included. For the rest of our stay, we used a public transport card in Montreal. We visited two provinces during this trip: Quebec and Ontario. If you want, you can also find the **"Ontario Province"** eguide in the same collection.

Speed limits:

In Canada, speed limits are as follows:

☞ In school areas in most provinces, the speed limit is 30 km/h during drop-off and child pickup, as well as around most urban parks.

☞ In urban areas, the speed limit is 50 km/h (70 km/h on some major roads).

☞ On provincial roads, the speed limit generally ranges from 70 to 100 km/h (90 in Quebec and Ontario).

☞ On motorways, the speed limit is between 60 and 100 km/h, or 110 km/h in some provinces such as Alberta, New Brunswick, Nova Scotia, Saskatchewan and Manitoba or 120 km/h in British Columbia.

Other features of the traffic in Canada:

Right turn on red light

It is generally allowed throughout Canada, EXCEPT on the island of Montreal and at intersections where there is a prohibition sign. When you want to turn right on red light, you have obligations to pedestrians. Before turning right at a red light, full stop is required. For more information about traffic, but also for different types of rental car, camping-cars, etc. here is a very useful site https://www.authentikcanada.com/holidays. You also have very nice routes ideas.

Accommodation

You have plenty of choices in terms of accommodation. Everything depends on your budget. For families travelling with children the cheapest variant in Canada consists of university residences, which are transformed during the holidays in residential hotels. The price of this kind of accommodation is cheaper than hotel rooms. We have successfully tested this kind of residence in the city center of Ottawa. Very convenient! We had an apartment with 2 bedrooms, bathroom and kitchen and paid for 4 nights: CAD 297. Another university residence we tested is that of

Kitchener, out of the city center, quiet. For the same kind of apartment and with breakfast (basic) included, we paid for 7 nights: CAD 481. You also can rent a cottage - some interesting websites here https://www.cottagesincanada.com, another here https://www.cottages-canada.ca/ and an international one here https://www.homeaway.ca.

Restaurants and other practical tips

The cuisine of the country is interesting, but in fact we could not test it often, because of the high prices of local restaurants. Yet, we have enjoyed quite a lot the Japanese restaurants, excellent, especially the formula "*All you can eat*". A real treat! We tested the famous poutine, a bit too greasy for our taste. Pancakes with maple syrup - excellent!

Electricity: 110 volts. You will need an US plug adapter.

How to use the *eGuide*?

You've already read dozens of books or even travel guides in your life. They usually have a table of contents at the beginning and either an index, glossary or a credits section at the end.

The electronic version of this guide contains a lot of this information, but it also has an added bonus that will help you to quickly and intuitively mobilize the content and personalize your reading mode: it is a true digital touch-screen eBook, a kind of website that doesn't need an Internet connection. We organized this guide in a conventional way for those who want to read "normally" without asking any metaphysical or methodological questions: if you want, you can jump directly to "The places to visit". For the curious or "computer savvy", here are the three modes of navigation that we offer. You can always go back while reading using the button "Back" on your smartphone, tablet or touch screen computer.

A top horizontal menu with 3 icons

Your *eguide* has at the top-right hand corner of every page a horizontal menu bar with three round "floating" icons. They are tagged "GeoNAV", "PhotoNAV" and "IcoNAV". Each of their functions is described below. All underlined texts are hyperlinks: therefore, you can click on them. You can see colored thematic icons, in a square shape, with a pictogram inside. Here are some examples:

 These icons announce clearly and simply the points of interest which are present in

the respective section. The background color of the icons depends on the theme. You can see the details of these icons in the IcoNAV chapter. At the top right, you can see THREE round navigation icons with a dark pictogram inside. Here is a detailed explanation:

1. GeoNAV: a "classic" geographical exploration

In the electronic version, by clicking the hypertext link (or **hyperlink**) located immediately below this round compass-styled icon, you reach a "classic" view of the map, displaying **colored geographical areas** and **hyperlinks next to the map** that allow you to access the respective chapter with a simple click (a smaller geographical map of the general area). From here you can select and read about the different places of interest you want to find out about.

2. PhotoNAV: discover the locations by photos

In the electronic version, by clicking the hypertext link located immediately below this **round camera-styled icon**, you can view photos taken by me or made available by the authors on Wikipedia, whom I make reference to and thank at the end of the book, in order to discover the beauty of this country. So, if you like a picture, click on it (or on the hyperlink below) and go directly to the respective tourist attractions!

3. IcoNAV: choose your points of interest by icons

In the electronic version, by clicking the hypertext link (or hyperlink) located below this round question-mark styled icon on a black background, you'll view the list of all the points of interest, or "icons" presented in this e-guide. Within the "IcoNAV" chapter, you'll view the thematic icons, and for each of them, its respective list of attractions, listed as hyperlinks, which you can activate by clicking. It couldn't be any easier!

How to view the geographic maps?

In the electronic version, if you are not connected to the Internet and if your eBook reader allows it, you can zoom in (with your mouse wheel or by spreading two fingers apart on your touch screen device) because their resolution allows to do so. If you have Internet access you can also access the maps proposed by the website **"OpenStreetMap"** by clicking or touching on the hyperlink (circled here in red) located immediately below the respective map.

GeoNAV

In the electronic version, you can browse your *eGuide* by choosing your desired location on the map.

Quebec Region, 15 tourist sections

PhotoNAV

In the electronic version, you can browse your guide by choosing your desired photo and touch it with your finger in order to "jump" directly in the location where it was taken from!

My favorite photos

Château Frontenac   Brodeur Creek Waterfalls

| Canyon of St. Anne | Mauricie Park |

IcoNAV

In the electronic version, you can browse your guide by choosing your points of interest or hobbies by icons. In this paper version you can find the section in the table of contents.

General information icons

CRUSH
Quebec | Wendake | Montreal

CHILDREN: location for children Quebec | Wendake | Montreal | Laval | Gatineau

TRICK
Quebec | Trois-Rivières | Montreal
IMPRESSIONS
Mauricie National Park

"Water" icons

BATHING: Take your swimsuits! Trois-Rivières

BEACH
Montreal | Percé

BOAT Saguenay | Tadoussac | Mauricie National Park

KAYAK Wendake | Grands-Jardins | Tadoussac | Mauricie Park | Sherbrooke | Laval | Gatineau

"Culture" icons

ART-CULTURE
Quebec | Deschambault-Grondines | Trois-Rivières | Sherbrooke Montreal | Saint-Eustache | Laval
RUINS
Trois-Rivières

MUSEUM Quebec Val-Jalbert | Saguenay | Trois-Rivières | Sherbrooke | Montreal | Laval | Gatineau

ARCHITECTURE
Quebec | Wendake | Val-Jalbert | Saguenay Tadoussac | Deschambault-Grondines | Trois-Rivières | Sherbrooke | Montreal | Saint-Eustache | Laval | Gatineau

RELIGIOUS MONUMENT
Quebec | Saguenay | Tadoussac Deschambault-Grondines | Trois-Rivières | Sherbrooke | Montreal | Saint-Eustache | Percé

CASTLE Quebec

"Nature" icons

 WILDLIFE Quebec | Grands-Jardins | Saguenay | Tadoussac | Mauricie Park | Deschambault-Grondines | Trois-Rivières | Montreal | Gatineau | Percé

 NATURE Quebec | Wendake | Grands-Jardins | Mauricie National Park | Deschambault-Grondines | Trois-Rivières | Sherbrooke | Montreal | Gatineau

 GARDEN, PARK Quebec | Sherbrooke | Montreal | Laval

 NATURAL Quebec | Wendake | Grands-Jardins | Val-Jalbert | Saguenay | Tadoussac | Trois-Rivières | Percé

 HIKE Quebec | Wendake | Grands-Jardins | Val-Jalbert | Saguenay | Tadoussac | Mauricie Park | Deschambault-Grondines | Trois-Rivières | Sherbrooke | Laval | Gatineau | Percé

 FISHING Grands-Jardins | Mauricie National Park | Trois-Rivières

 LANDSCAPE Quebec | Wendake | Grands-Jardins | Saguenay | Tadoussac | Mauricie National Park | Deschambault-Grondines | Trois-Rivières | Montreal | Percé

"Sport" icons

 SKI Grands-Jardins

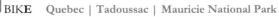 **CLIMBING** Quebec | Grands-Jardins National Park

 BIKE Quebec | Tadoussac | Mauricie National Park

"Leisure activities and life on-the-spot" icons

 ACCOMMODATION Wendake | Grands-Jardins | Val-Jalbert | Tadoussac | Mauricie Park | Trois-Rivières | Montreal | Gatineau | Percé

 BUDGET Quebec | Wendake | Grands-Jardins | Val-Jalbert | Saguenay | Tadoussac | Mauricie Park | Trois-Rivières | Montreal

 RESTAURANT Quebec | Wendake | Montreal | Gatineau

LEISURE PARK Quebec

 SHOPPING, SOUVENIRS Quebec | Wendake | Val-Jalbert | Montreal

 CASINO Gatineau

9

Province of Quebec

The Quebec Administrative Region or the Province of Quebec is divided into 17 administrative regions. Although there is not an elected political authority responsible for managing Canada's regions, they have an appointed responsible minister who deals with local issues with the rest of the government. We will mention in this guide the main tourist attractions of this province.

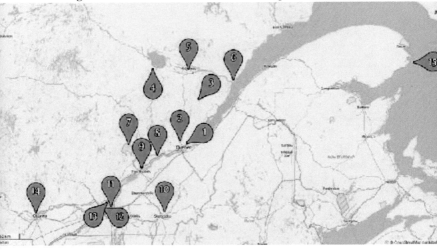

1. Quebec	2. Wendake	3. Grands-Jardins
4. Val-Jalber	5. Saguenay	6. Tadoussac
7. Mauricie Park	8. Deschambault-Grondines	
9. Trois-Rivières	10. Sherbrooke	11. Montreal
12. Saint-Eustache	13. Laval	14. Gatineau 15. Percé

1. Quebec

Quebec is the capital of the province of the same name, located in eastern Canada. It is located on the banks of the St. Lawrence River and was founded in 1608. The name of the town comes from the Algonquin word meaning "where the river narrows", referring to the narrowing of St. Lawrence River between the cities of Quebec and Lévis. The Old-Quebec was listed as UNESCO World Heritage and filled with treasures: fortifications, museums and small charming districts. Although it is a city full of tourists, I found it much less hectic than Montreal or Toronto... If you want peace, visit early in the morning, before 10am since after this time, the buses start dropping off hundreds of tourists of all nationalities!

   Quebec is the city we loved the most

during our travel. It is a provincial city with a warm and intimate atmosphere. Old Quebec is picturesque and walking in the alleys full of life is a real pleasure.

Photo 1.1: Royal Place in old Quebec

Photo 1.2: Alley of old Quebec

If you want to have a glimpse of the city before starting to visit it in detail, you can take a red open roof bus that circles the old Quebec. There are 12 stops: ***Place d'Armes*** where you can see the Fort Museum and the Museum of French America; ***Nouvo St-Roch District*** with shops and trendy restaurants; ***Museum of Civilization***, ***Place Royale*** where you can make a visit to the "Interpretation Center of Place Royale", to "Our Lady of Victories" and "Chevalier House"; ***Market of the Old-Port***, ***Convention Center***, ***Observatory of the Capital*** with the Parliament Building, the Tourny Fountain and the Promenade of Prime ministers; ***Armory*** with the Discovery Pavilion; ***Plains of Abraham*** to enjoy the Citadel, the Remains of the Blockhouse and the Promenade of Governors; ***Museum of Fine Arts*** with Jeanne d'Arc's Gardens and Martello Towers to see; ***Place d'Youville*** with the Montcalm Palace, Capitol and Canada Park and finally the **Quebec Citadel** with the Esplanade Park. The price is 36 CAD/person (approx. 26€) 22 CAD/child and 113.80 CAD (82€) for a family of 2 adults + 2 children. For details see their website.

Photo 1.4: Citadel of old Quebec~

Photo 1.5: Dufferin Terrace

You can start your adventure through Old Quebec and Artillery Park. This fortress was of great strategic importance and surveyed the plateau to the west, where an army could besiege the city. It overlooks the St. Charles River, where ships could disembark. The French, British and Canadians have followed throughout history by taking advantage of these fortifications. You can choose to visit on your own or take a guided tour. For all the details see their website here https://www.pc.gc.ca/en/lhn-nhs/qc/fortifications. The historic site **"Fortifications of Quebec"** ensures the protection and enhancement of the walls and gates of the city of Quebec, to the Governors' Garden and Montmorency

Park, Dufferin Terrace and the Governors' promenade. The fortifications surround the Upper Town on almost 5 kilometers and the itinerary is really interesting. They have a star shape, characteristic of Vauban styled fortifications and offer spectacular views of the city and the river.

Photo 1.7: Frontenac castle seen from the Plains of Abraham

Less than 3 km south along the river, you will discover a beautiful historic park: **The park of Champs-de-Bataille**, gathering the Plains of Abraham and The Braves Park, built to honor the memory of French and English combatants. It plays the role of an urban park nowadays, a real lung of the city with a hundred hectares of greenery, flowered and wooded plains and hills. It is a place frequented not only by the tourists but also by Quebecers. Enjoy nature by walking on the trails in the arboretum or the Jeanne d'Arc Garden. For details see here http://www.lesplainesdabraham.ca/en/ Located at the entrance of the park, the **Discovery Pavilion** allows to plan a visit. A beautiful model of the plains, as well as the Odyssey multimedia exhibition are just as many pretexts of visit. In addition, you will find information on activities taking place in the park, a gift shop, a tourist information desk, an Internet station and a currency exchange.

On the way, admire the magnificent Parliament Building that houses the National Assembly of Quebec. The architectural complex is a beauty to behold, in New-Renaissance style with mansard roofs and statues. It traces the history of Quebec. Above the main door is carved the Quebec coat of arms and motto of the city: « *Je me souviens* » (I remember).

Photo 1.8: Parliament Building

In the middle of the **Parc des Champs-de-Bataille** there is a museum not to be missed for art lovers: the **National Museum of Fine Arts of Quebec** sheltering tens of thousands of works illustrating Quebec art. For all the details see their website.

Not far away, on the river shore, stroll in the Sillery district. The *Grande Allée* is one of the most famous streets in Quebec, parallel to St. Lawrence River and going through the district. Maguire Avenue is lined with houses and charming shops. There are several historic houses with gardens to visit in the neighborhood: **The Cataraqui Domain, Villa Bagatelle** - a representative example of the influence of English Picturesque style in Quebec. Another beautiful park is that of Bois-de-Coulonge, located on the hill of Quebec and overlooking St. Lawrence River. On the way of the Foulon along the river, near the Samuel of Champlain promenade, is the Jesuit house of Sillery, a historic building from the XVIIIth century.

Photo 1.9: Frontenac castle as seen from Levis

A magnificent castle not to be missed on the Dufferin Terrace is the **Château Frontenac** majestically overlooking the river. Difficult indeed not to notice because of its imposing size!!! It overlooks the cap Diamant and is bordered to the north by the St. Louis Street and to the south by Mount Carmel Street. This castle is the first of a long series of luxury hotels built by Canadian railways in the late XIXth century and early XXth century to popularize train travel. It was built in several stages and has five wings and a central tower. The best views to photograph it is the terrace of Lévis, Quebec's Citadel or the observatory of the building Marie-Guyart. The architecture of the castle is impressive with massive towers, circular and polygonal turrets, copper roofs, gables and dormers, false battlements. To learn all the details of this castle or book a room in the Hotel, see their website here https://www.fairmont.com/frontenac-quebec/.

Photo 1.11: Petit-Champlain district - beautiful fresco near the funicular

Photo 1.12: Alley of the Funicular

A funicular connects the Upper and Lower Town. The access is by Dufferin Terrace, right behind the Frontenac Castle and the funicular will take you to the Louis Jolliet, located in the Petit-Champlain district.

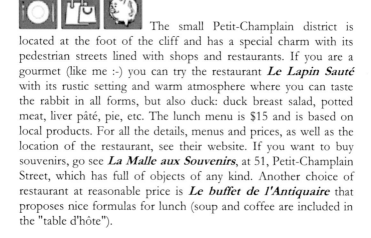 The small Petit-Champlain district is located at the foot of the cliff and has a special charm with its pedestrian streets lined with shops and restaurants. If you are a gourmet (like me :-) you can try the restaurant *Le Lapin Sauté* with its rustic setting and warm atmosphere where you can taste the rabbit in all forms, but also duck: duck breast salad, potted meat, liver pâté, pie, etc. The lunch menu is $15 and is based on local products. For all the details, menus and prices, as well as the location of the restaurant, see their website. If you want to buy souvenirs, go see *La Malle aux Souvenirs*, at 51, Petit-Champlain Street, which has full of objects of any kind. Another choice of restaurant at reasonable price is *Le buffet de l'Antiquaire* that proposes nice formulas for lunch (soup and coffee are included in the "table d'hôte").

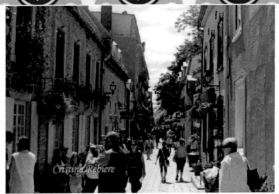

Photo 1.16: Petit-Champlain district - charming alleys

Photo 1.17: City hall of Quebec

The most impressive church in Quebec is perhaps the ***Basilique Notre Dame de Quebec***, in front of the city hall. Repeatedly destroyed and rebuilt, the current church dates from 1930. Steps of the Holy Door, there is the **Museum of French America**, which traces the history of French culture in North America and abroad up until today. For all the details see the website.

The Heritage site Beauport extends on about six kilometers and offers magnificent views of St. Lawrence River and Orleans Island. The Royal Road and Royal Avenue are lined with beautiful buildings that reflect the architecture of the XVIIIth to XXth century. The historic center of Beauport is actually the district Old-Bourg where you can see the magnificent church *Église de la Nativité-de-Notre-Dame*.

Photo 1.18: Montmorency fall

 For lovers of nature and beautiful falls, don't miss the **Montmorency Fall Park** which is located on the edge of the district of the same name belonging to the Beauport site, at the mouth of the river. It is a beautiful site, with a fall of 83 meters high, 30 meters higher than Niagara Falls! For those who like mountain climbing or want to try a via ferrata, don't hesitate because you will see the waterfall from a completely different angle! As for other thrills, there is also a double zip line... For the less adventurous there are walks and hiking trails, including one not to be missed along the cliff. On the suspension bridge you'll hear the rumbling fall under your feet... and you can admire the panorama. For those who prefer biking, there are two bike trails and you can rent bikes by having an interesting package in conjunction with the cable car here https://locationechosports.ca/eindex.php.html.

For all the details on the activities and prices of the park see here https://www.sepaq.com/destinations/parc-chute-montmorency/.

If you visit Quebec during the summer, you will be able to see *The Festival of New France* celebrating for five days the history of the first European settlers in America. On the program: dance, shows and parades. And if you are going during winter, there is the carnival with shows, dog sled rides, a village for children, etc.

If you are traveling with children, a visit that will make them happy is to the Aquarium of Quebec where they can admire fish, reptiles, polar bears, walruses and seals.

Photo 1.19: Galleries of the capital

They can also do tree climbing and many other discovery activities. If the weather is bad another way to amuse children is the **Galleries of the Capital**, a shopping mall that shelters an amusement park and plenty of shops. Avoid Sundays when it is pure madness... :-)

My gourmand crush was in Levis: a restaurant that hides its charm "L'intimiste". Reasonable prices and great formulas for lunch including soup and dessert. Delicious pumpkin soup and terrific angus steak in an exquisite sauce with excellent homemade French fries and will make you surely come back!!!

Photo 1.22: Le plumard - very good accommodation near Quebec

We chose to live in an apartment located in a *bed & breakfast* in Levis: "Le plumard". Anne is an excellent host and the apartment was nice, with everything you need, even a washing machine and a dryer which greatly facilitates life during long trips! We paid 475 CAD for 9 days which is a good price for Canada! We recommend you warmly "Le plumard"!

44 km north of Quebec, there is a beautiful natural site to see: the canyon of Sainte-Anne. Its magnificent fall of 74 meters is a tourist attraction in the region. There is a beautiful hike in the woods which allows the view of the waterfall from all angles. You can go climbing or simply enjoy the scenery. To avoid the crowds, go early in the morning.

Photo 1.23: Canyon of Sainte-Anne

2. Wendake

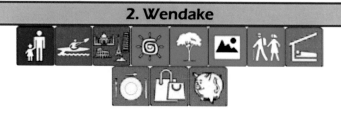

Wendake is a Huron-Wendat Indian Reserve from the Quebec province, located 15 km northwest of Quebec, on the St. Charles River.

You can start your visit with the old Wendake, south, with 300-year-old houses, small craft shops and some restaurants. However, do not be surprised that it is small :-)! We asked locals where the old center was, but they looked at us strangely... The Huron-Wendat community was founded in 1697 and the Indians are from Georgian Bay, located southeast of Lake Huron in Ontario, where their main area of population was. If you want to taste indigenous specialties, you have several famous restaurants such as the *Sagamité*, whose name comes from the soup-meal made with squash, corn and red beans that Indians cultivated and enriched with game they hunted. You can treat yourself with bison or boar, rabbit or elk, pheasant or doe, but also taste their soups and pastries. For more details see their website here https://www.sagamite.com/accueil.aspx. Another nice restaurant is **La Traite** that offers traditional dishes at reasonable prices: for lunch you have a special formula with dishes around 15 euros together with the soup of the day, dessert and coffee/herbal tea included in the price. If you go on Sunday, don't miss their brunch that costs 29$/adult and 14.5$/child!

Photo 2.2: Wendake - restaurant Sagamité

Photo 2.1: Old house in Wendake

Photo 2.3: Wendake - Kabir Kouba waterfall

     For nature and hiking lovers, you should go see the ***Parc linéaire de la rivière St-Charles***, which is a trail of 32 km along the St. Charles River, from its mouth up to its source, at Lake St. Charles. This walk passes through the community of Wendake and you can admire a multitude of landscapes, historical sites, cross bridges or wooden paths above the water, enjoy the wilderness, etc. Children can have fun on the playground on the banks or water games during the summer. In the Park "Les Saules" you'll discover a rich flora, with ferns, spring trills and large willows and observe lots of birds. One of the most beautiful areas is that of the Kabir Kouba fall. If you want a guided tour or enjoy a canoe ride, see this website https://www.chutekabirkouba.com/.

If you want to rent a canoe, a kayak or a rabaska for several persons, you will find here https://canotslegare.com/. The canoe area is in the Water Tower Area and the Meanders section of the park above.

Photo 2.5: Wendake

If you want to stay in the reserve or have more details on the things to see and do in Wendake, visit this website here https://tourismewendake.ca/en/.

3. Grands-Jardins National Park

Grands-Jardins is a national park in the Quebec province, located 130 km north of the capital of this region. It stretches over 300 km² and offers beautiful scenery of taiga and tundra.

Photo 3.2: Grands-Jardins National Park

One of the reasons for the existence of this park is the presence of a herd of woodland caribou and spruce-lichen. You may be lucky to see one of them, but also other animals such as black bear, moose, otter, beaver, lynx, wolf, etc. The park has a trail network of over 30 km for hikers, in all categories. You'll discover lots of different landscapes: taiga, tundra, deciduous forest, boreal forest. One of the most beautiful hikes is that of Mount Swan Lake, but with a fairly high level of difficulty, on 8.4 km and will take you about 4 hours: unique perspective on the meteorite crater of Charlevoix and on the Gros-Bras valley. An easier hike where you can discover the flora and fauna of the taiga is the *Le Boréal* Path, a 2 km loop that lasts about one hour.

The price of admission in Canadian national parks is 8.5 CAD (6 €) for an adult and free for children and young people under 18 years old.

If you want to rent a canoe, a kayak or a rabaska for several people, you will find on location and you can rent the boat by hour or for a day. Rental must be made to the service center of the Mont-du-Lac-des-Cygnes (21st km) or at the center of discovery and Arthabaska services. The trip on the water is calm, on the lake Arthabaska towards the dam Wabano.

If you like climbing, don't miss the via ferrata of the park that you can do with a guide. For the details on the prices of services and activities offered in the park see here https://www.sepaq.com/pq/grj/index.dot?language_id=1.

For fishing lovers, you can take advantage of the "day fishing" prices. Lakes Carré, des Castors, Pemmican, Chaudière, des Îles and Turgeon are full of speckled trout. A boat is provided on these six outstanding lakes to learn how to fish. You can also enjoy fishing packages with accommodation or camping. For the prices and details see the park's website.

If you go during the cold season, there is a Nordic ski trail that crosses a spruce forest and borrows the park roads. The trails are marked. You can stop on shelters of Lake Pointu, accessible every day. Another winter activity is the "ice fishing" on the lake Étang-Malbaie in February and March.

4. Val-Jalbert

Val-Jalbert is an ancient village of Quebec, located 250 km north of the capital. Its territory is part of the municipality of Chambord, at Lac-Saint-Jean and it was turned into a tourist attraction in the 1960s.

This village will immerse you in the Canada of the 1920s. It is an open-air museum where you can admire the antique wooden houses, the convent-school, the post office and the general store transformed today in a gift shop. You can also visit the mini power plant that produces electricity using the river fall.

The price of admission is 26.96 CAD (approx. 20 €) for adults, 13.70 CAD (10 €) for children and free for children

under 6. If you want to stay in the village, you'll have reduced prices for the entrance or even included in the package. For accommodation in an antique house, camping or mini-chalet see here https://www.valjalbert.com/en/rates/hebergement

Photo 4.2: Ouiatchouan waterfall, Val Jalbert

If you want to go hiking, there is a canyon trail along the river Ouiatchouan. The fall of the river is 74 meters high and if you still have energy, by climbing up the stairs you'll reach the second fall, the Maligne fall about fifty meters high.

5. Saguenay

Saguenay is a city of Quebec, located 210 km north of the capital. It extends from the north shore of the Saguenay River to the Laurentian mountain, upstream of the Saguenay Fjord and downstream of the Horst of Kénogami. This is actually a metropolis that includes several cities.

You can start your visit by the city center of Chicoutimi where you can admire the Cathedral Saint-François-Xavier de Chicoutimi, built in 1922 in Renaissance style mixed with Roman style.

Photo 5.1: Chicoutimi

A museum not to be missed in town is the **Pulperie de Chicoutimi**, located on the banks of the river of the same name. This company mechanically transformed the wood into paper pulp in the early XXth century. The entry price is 14.5 CAD/adult and 6.5 CAD/child. There are several buildings to visit: St. Joseph mill, the oldest, built on Electric Island and connected to the shore by a bridge over one of the two arms of the river; Mill St. Mary built in 1903 after the success that the company obtained in 1900 at the Universal Exposition in Paris - this was the largest mill in North America at the time and it allowed to triple the production. As demand has grown steadily, a third mill was built in the same style of an "industrial cathedral". In July 1996, a major flood has almost completely destroyed the site, which was subsequently rebuilt. Currently the museum houses thousands of historical objects and several exhibitions on the themes of art and history. Not far from the pulp factory is *"The small White House"*, in the Basin district which was the only one to withstand the torrential rainfall Saguenay flood in 1996. It became a symbol of the tragedy that struck the community that year.

Photo 5.2: Pulp factory of Chicoutimi

A great visit not to be missed is that of the Saguenay Fjord. You can take a boat to visit the Bagotville Dock of Saguenay or the shuttle that transports you from towns to villages on the Saguenay Fjord at fixed hours. All along the river you can admire magnificent landscapes of the cliffs of Cape Trinity and Cape Eternity lying near the village of Sainte-Rose-du-Nord. The fjord holds a deep gash in the Laurentians, bordered by steep cliffs, a hundred kilometers long and with a width varying from 1 to 3.5 km. The majestic gorges are the result of the last glaciation and there is a moraine at the mouth of the St. Lawrence River, creating a high background. It was then invaded by the sea after the melting of glaciers. For prices and details see their website here. The Saguenay fjord is protected and highlighted by two parks: Saguenay National Park and Saguenay-Saint-Laurent Marine Park.

 The **Saguenay National park** will delight lovers of gorgeous landscapes. Cruises are available between June and October in Rivière-Éternité costing 55 CAD/adult and 27 CAD/child and free for children less than 5 years old. The cruise lasts 1h30.

For a cheaper price you can discover the fjord in zodiac. If you want to know the price of all activities in the park see here https://www.sepaq.com/pq/sag/tarifs.dot. For those who enjoy hiking, there are several trails of all levels. The easiest is the *Trail of the Méandres-à-Falaises*, a loop of less than 2 km that will take you about forty minutes. Another hike, with a much higher difficulty is the *Falls Trail* with a length of 5 km up to the first fall – you'll have a beautiful view over the fjord and the village of Anse-Saint-Jean. For the most courageous, you can continue up to the top of the White Mountain, the highest accessible summit of the park, where you'll have a spectacular panorama.

Another beautiful trail that goes along the coastline and through a nice pine forest, from where the panorama of the fjord looks magnificent is the *Pine Trail*. Forest and marine environments generate astonishing biodiversity: wolves, black bears, lynx, beavers and moose can be spotted with a bit of luck in the forests of the park, while the seals, whales and other marine mammals can be seen from the banks.

6. Tadoussac

Tadoussac is a village in Quebec, located 217 km northeast of the capital, on the edge of St. Lawrence River, at the mouth of the Saguenay River. It has many touristic attractions.

 In this village there is the chapel of Tadoussac, the oldest wooden chapel of Canada. It dates from 1747. For more information about the history of this church, but also the surroundings, consult the site here http://www.chapelledetadoussac.com/.

Photo 6.1: Chapel of Tadoussac

      The Hotel Tadoussac is also of architectural interest, in Anglo-Norman style, with its red roof that attracts all the attention. It offers several packages for whale watching, including the rorqual and sometimes the blue whale, but also bike or kayak packages. For all the details visit their website here https://www.hoteltadoussac.com/en/.

7. Mauricie National Park

The **Mauricie National Park**, located in the region of the same name, in the province of Quebec, is 150 km west of the capital. It stretches over 500 km² and offers beautiful landscapes with more than a hundred lakes, majestic forests and a surprising nature. This is the most beautiful national park that we visited in both provinces! It is accessible from the villages of Saint-Jean-des-Piles and Saint-Mathieu-du-Parc.

Photo 7.1: Trail *La cache* on the shore of *Lac du fou*

The landscapes of this park are typically Canadian: forests, lakes, hills. Enjoy many trails of all difficulty setting to admire the beauty of the scenery, throughout seasons and you may even get the chance to see a moose, a beaver, a black bear, a red fox, a lynx, a raccoon, a porcupine or a marmot. There are over 200 species of birds on its territory. A good observation point is at La Cache at the shore of lake Lac du Fou where you'll find a telescope for this purpose. If you like the flora, don't miss the small walk La Tourbière that is done on a wooden path, in the middle of a "carpet" of floating vegetation where there are fascinating orchids and even carnivorous plants. The Lac-Étienne Trail is also very nice with observatories, interpretation panels and a telescope to observe the birds. A little longer hike, of

8.3 km that will take you 4 hours is that of Ruisseau-Bouchard that starts at Solitaire lake and offers magnificent panoramas.

Photo 7.2: La Tourbière

The price of admission in Canadian national parks is 8.5 CAD (6€) for an adult and free for children and teens under 18 years old.

A very beautiful trail is that of the **Ruisseau Brodeur** that you can combine with those of the **Falaises**. These are two wonderful walks in the forest, along the waterfalls where a lot of Canadians come and cool off during the summer. You can then go up the cliffs where you can admire the stunning landscapes. These are two hiking loops that are really great!!!

Photo 7.5: Étienne Lake

Photo 7.7: Ruisseau Brodeur

If you want to rent a canoe or a kayak, you'll find on site, by hour or by day, on Shewenegan, Wapizagonke or Lake Edward picnic areas. To see the prices, visit their website. If you like wild camping, you can do it in this park, from mid-May to mid-October. For the details on pricing, regulations and other useful information, see here https://www.pc.gc.ca/en/pn-np/qc/mauricie/activ/.

For fishing enthusiasts, you can take advantage of the "day fishing" prices. To fish in the park, you have to provide a special permit from the National Park of Mauricie. You can also benefit from fishing packages with accommodation or camping. For prices and details see here https://www.sepaq.com/pq/grj/.

If you like mountain biking, a network of 55 km with rest stops awaits you in the heart of the forest in the Mauricie National Park. Rent a bike at the service pavilion. To obtain the trail map and other details see here https://www.pc.gc.ca/en/pn-np/qc/mauricie/activ.

Photo 7.11: Magnificent panorama of Mauricie park

Photo 7.13: Hike in the Mauricie Park

This national park has a unique atmosphere. The forests are majestic and hiking in the woods is so charming... It's like an elven world... I made hundreds of photos there, completely conquered by the beautiful trees, the stones covered with moss, magnificent ferns, mushrooms that delight the eyes, the faults in the rock walls that feed the imagination of the walker, tree trunks on which grows an entire vegetal universe... It was so impressive to me that, walking through these forests, along waterfalls and cliffs, I imagined the action of one of the episodes of my series for children "Cathy Merlin". It even was during our trip to Canada that I wrote the second of the series: "Cathy Merlin 2. *Le sentier des secrets*". At the end of this second volume, Cathy is going in this Mauricie National Park that impressed me so much. I also wrote

the third episode, the action happens entirely in Canada: "Cathy Merlin 3. Les Canadelfes" ;-)

Deschambault-Grondines is a municipality of Quebec, created in 2002 by the fusion of the two villages. It is located 62 km southwest of Quebec, on the St. Lawrence River.

You can start your visit with the ancient village Deschambault and its St. Joseph's Church, built in 1835, stone made. Its architecture is quite curious: built on a Latin cross plan consisting of a three-nave, canted transept, a choir finished in an apse with rounded corners and a facade with a hipped gable adorned with a statue of St. Joseph. In the other village, there is also a beautiful church with its adjacent cemetery: St. Charles-Borromée Church. The rectory of St. Charles-des-Grondines is also to be seen, built in 1843 in Neoclassical style.

Photo 8.1: Saint-Joseph church

To the west of the village is an interesting building: *Le Moulin de La Chevrotière*, built in 1802. It houses an Adokwané exhibition that tells the history of the site before the arrival of Europeans. For more details see http://grandquebec.com/capitale-quebec/deschambault. Another tourist attraction is in Grondines: the Moulin banal de Grondines (banal mill of Grondines). It's a windmill, built in 1674, consisting of a white cylindrical tower with three floors topped by a conical roof. An exhibition on the history of the village is housed in this building.

9. Trois-Rivières

Trois-Rivières is a city of Quebec province at the mouth of the Saint-Maurice River. It is located 130 km south of Quebec on the St. Lawrence River. The name of the city is actually an optical illusion, which refers to the three channels that the Saint-Maurice River forms at its mouth with the St. Lawrence between two islands: the Potherie and Saint-Quentin islands.

Photo 9.3: Armory of Trois-Rivières

One of the most impressive churches in the city is the Notre-Dame-du-Cap basilica, located at Cap-de-la-Madeleine. It is dedicated to the Virgin Mary and welcomes thousands of pilgrims every year. The original chapel dates from 1717, but the current structure dates from 1955. A large statue of Mary adorns its facade and its architectural style surprises with its octagonal shape and its pyramid-shaped dome. Its height is about 80 meters. The interior is harmonious, without column to block the view, with large arches and beautiful stained-glass windows.

16 km northwest of the basilica, you'll find a national historic site: Les Forges du Saint-Maurice. The site is located along the river of the same name. The natural setting is in tune with the history of this place that speaks of a time when a whole community was beating to the rhythm of the steel production. In addition to the multimedia show, visit the key points of this place: the blast furnace, the big house, that once served as a residence, store and warehouse that now shelters exhibitions on the history of the forges. Along the creek that runs through the site, there are vestiges of the upper forge, the grist mill and the wood mill. If you wish a walk in the surroundings, the nature trail laid out along the St. Maurice River offers beautiful landscapes. The entrance fee is quite low: 3.90 CAD/adult and 1.90 CAD/child. For more information see their website here https://www.pc.gc.ca/fr/lhn-nhs/qc/saintmaurice/index.

One of the most interesting streets of the town is the Ursulines Street. All along there are historical homes, but also museums: The Tonnancour Manor is a building located at n° 864, that shelters the art gallery park with exhibitions of paintings, drawings, prints, photos, videos, sculptures and media. Another museum is the Ursuline Museum which was the first hospital in the city and presents through thousands of objects the history of the community and the evolution of the city and region. Another museum located in an imposing building looking like a red brick castle is the Armory of Trois-Rivières, in the Saint-François-Xavier street. It was built in 1906 on two floors and has four towers aliasing two rounds at the ends of the facade and two polygonal framing the entrance. In the same street, at n°732, you'll see the Philip Verrette house, in "Boomtown" style. The Boomtown architecture style appears in North America towards the end of the XIXth century and the beginning of the XXth century by presenting a simple and economical solution to an increased demand for housing. The plan is cubic with one or two floors.

If you like history and nature, you can combine both by visiting the Moulin seigneurial de Pointe-du-Lac, located 17 km south of the city, by the river, it includes a flour mill dating from the seigneurial period and a sawmill built in the mid-XXth century. Several hiking trails crisscross over 10 km and let you admire the architectural ensemble, go along and cross the St. Charles River and see the channel of lords. At thirty kilometers northeast of Trois-Rivières, by the river, there is the Old Presbytery of Batiscan, dating back to the XIXth century: a haven where you can enjoy the historical and birds interpretation trails. Another interesting site is located within 13 km to the north, still by the river: The Sainte-Anne seigneurial Domain and its beautiful gardens. If you decide to visit the three sites you can get a discounted price of 7.00 CAD with the trio Card, instead of 3.50 CAD for each site...

     At 50 km west of Trois-Rivières is the beautiful **St. Ursule's Waterfalls Park** open from May to October. You'll enjoy hiking trails, admire the falls of 70 meters and even rent a cottage on site if you so wish. At sixty kilometers north of Trois-Rivières is the magnificent Mauricie Park with gorgeous landscapes of forests, lakes and hills, numerous trails, rich flora and fauna. For all the details and activities see the dedicated section.

 A hundred kilometers northwest of Trois-Rivières is the **Wildlife Mastigouche** with superb landscapes. For fishing lovers, there are more than a hundred lakes and interesting fishing-hosting packages. There are some hiking trails of all levels of difficulty. I recommend "The Chicot", a 2 km trail that offers stunning panoramas. From June to September, you can swim at the patrolled beach of Lake St. Bernard. There are several types of accommodation available on site: camping, cottages or Ready-to-camp Tent Hékipia. For the prices see on their website.

10. Sherbrooke

Sherbrooke is a city of Quebec, located at the confluence of the Magog and St. Francis rivers, in the administrative region of Estrie. It is about 150 kilometers east of Montreal and the same distance south of Trois-Rivières. Its hilly region is very touristic.

Photo 10.1: Basilica Saint-Michel

In the city center of Sherbrooke there is the Saint-Michel Cathedral Basilica, in Gothic style. Its architecture is inspired by the Notre Dame of Paris. It was built on the heights of the Saint-Michel cliff in 1915. The tower housing the bell has a height of nearly 80 meters.

For art lovers, not far from the basilica, across the river, there is the **Sherbrooke Museum of Fine Arts** with three exhibition rooms dedicated to the art of the Eastern regions. For all the details see their website here http://mbas.qc.ca/en/home/.

17 km north of the museum you can see a beautiful building: the City Hall of Sherbrooke, built in 1904 in Second Empire style.

4 km south of Saint-Michel Cathedral-Basilica is the largest city park that extends over 200 hectares: Mont-Bellevue's Park. It includes the John S. Bourque and Bellevue Mountains. You can go hiking and do archery during the summer. There is also a small ski center. For the map of hiking trails, see here https://www.ville.sherbrooke.qc.ca/en/

Five kilometers to the north there is another park, the Lucien-Blanchard Park, on the banks of the Magog River. You can rent pedal boats, kayaks, electric boats at the Water House.

11. Montreal

Montreal is located in the south of the province of Quebec, and it is its main metropolis. It is the most populous French-speaking city in America and also one of the largest French-speaking cities in the world. It is located 260 km southwest of Quebec. The city lies on Montreal Island, in the Archipelago of Hochelaga, at the confluence of the St. Lawrence River and the Ottawa River, near Ontario and the United States. This is a metropolis full of contrasts where different cultures blend harmoniously, which makes its unique charm. It takes several days to visit all the treasures of Montreal. At least five or six. We spent six, but we would gladly return there!

You'll easily fall in love with Montreal because its charm comes from a subtle blend of old Europe with modern America. If you visit the city at least for three days, then you can save money by purchasing the Museums Pass with 3 days transports that will cost you 80 CAD only and will entitle you to free entry in a lot of museums and tourist attractions to visit in Montreal, as well as unlimited travel with bus and subway! For all the details and to buy it, see here. Otherwise, the Montreal Passport we talked about in the introduction is also a good alternative. It's up to you to choose the one that best suits your needs and your stay.

In the city center, Mount Royal is a hill that dominates the surrounding plain with three peaks. This is the *Central Park* of Montreal that is actually called **Mount Royal Park**. A major attraction is the Beaver Lake, an artificial basin with shallow water that turns into an ice rink during the winter. This is a nice walking area. People are jogging, biking or enjoying a picnic. To admire the scenery, you will find the Kondiaronk scenic

lookout in front of the Mount Royal chalet that offers a full panorama of the skyscrapers of the city center and the St. Lawrence River. The Duluth Avenue connects the Mount Royal Park at Lafontaine's one, by crossing the borough Le Plateau-Mont-Royal. This is an avenue full of restaurants and shops, with beautiful houses.

Photo 11.3: McGill University

For art lovers, east of Mount Royal, there is a

museum that is worth a visit: The Museum of Fine Arts. It is located in Sherbrooke West Street and hosts fashion shows, fine arts, music, design, archeology, photography, Quebec and international art, etc. For all the details about the exhibitions, prices and schedules see their website here https://www.mbam.qc.ca/en/. Another museum to visit is The Museum of Contemporary Art, the largest of its kind in Canada, which is located in Sainte-Catherine Street.

 St. Catherine Street is an ideal place for shopping: full of shops, small restaurants and cafes. Going up the street you will reach the Place Ville Marie where several buildings are located, including a huge mall with 75 shops, cafes and restaurants. For the details see here. On the esplanade, the view of McGill College Avenue extends to the campus of McGill University. Nearby there is the fountain sculpture entitled Female Landscape which is the work of Gerald Gladstone.

By continuing 2 km north, you'll begin to discover Old Montreal with its European charm. You willl pass next to the magnificent Notre-Dame Basilica, built in 1824, in Neo-Gothic style. Don't hesitate to enter to discover its beautiful wooden setting and stained glass. On the Place d'Armes, there is a small park and in the center is the Maisonneuve's Monument, in memory of one of the city founders. North of the square you'll find the Bank of Montreal in Neo-classical style, inspired by the Roman Pantheon, with a Corinthian colonnade, a triangular pediment and a dome whose gilded interior ceilings are impressive. There is a museum inside that traces the history of the bank. To the east of the square there is the Aldred Building, a 23-floors-skyscraper, built in 1929 in Art Deco style. Right next to it, another building, the New York Life Building, the first skyscraper in Canada, built in 1889. It is on this square that you can see the Old Saint-Sulpice Seminary, a XVIIth century building with its gardens, a lawn and a central statue. The geometrical arrangement of the alleys recalls the Renaissance style of French gardens. Following on Notre Dame Street, a few hundred meters away there is another beautiful square: Jacques-Cartier, lined with beautiful houses, cafes and restaurants.

Photo 11.4: Place d'Armes

Another museum to see if you like history is Pointe-à-Callière, a museum of archeology and history of Montreal. The museum entrance is marked by the Spur, a triangular building with a tower overlooking the port of Montreal. For all the details on the many museum collections, prices and schedules, see here https://pacmusee.qc.ca/en/. The entry price is 20 CAD/adult and 7 CAD/child. One kilometer away there is another museum: the *Château Ramezay*. This large villa was the residence of the governor and is surrounded by a beautiful little French garden: a vegetable garden, a flower garden and another with herbs. For all the details see the website here. https://www.chateauramezay.qc.ca/en/. The title of "castle" is not really suited, because it's just a small manor. Charming inside, it's true. Just in front of the house, you will not miss the City Hall, a Second Empire style building.

Photo 11.7: Ramezay castle

Photo 11.8: Bonsecours Market

A few hundred meters further is the Bonsecours Market, easily recognizable by its imposing silver dome. It shelters exclusive boutiques, cafes and restaurants.
For all the details see here their website http://www.marchebonsecours.qc.ca/fr/boutiques.html.

Just off the market Bonsecours there is the **Notre-Dame-de-Bon-Secours**, a pilgrimage church that is located in Saint-Paul Street. The construction of this church began in 1655. At the back of the chapel, there is a statue of the Virgin Mary that overlooks the harbor. This statue is also known as The Sea Star because it is crowned with a starry halo and open arms to welcome the sailors. Feel free to go up the street of the Commune, which runs along the Old Port of Montreal.

Photo 11.9: Notre-Dame-de-Bon-Secours

The old port is located on the north bank of the St. Lawrence River and extends over two kilometers from McGill Street up to Amherst Street from where you can see the clock tower. This tower was built in 1921, in memory of the sailors of the merchant marine who died during the First World War. It has a beautiful clock and a lamp guiding the ships. The old port is a lively place, with cafes, shops and exuberant nightlife. The Clock Beach is a place very frequented by tourists, with its fine sand, chairs, parasols and mist generators.

If you have children or if you are a science lover, don't forget to go to the Montreal Science Center in the heart of the Old Port of Montreal. Young and old will be amazed by the exhibits that help you explore, learn and understand diverse topics related to science and technology. There are several organized workshops with challenges for the whole family. For all the details see their website here https://www.montrealsciencecentre.com/.

Photo 11.12: Montreal Science Center

A few hundred meters further, on Place d'Youville, there is the Montreal History Center, in a former fire station, built in 1903. It's a beautiful red brick building, in Dutch style with many influences, surrounded by a square tower with a hipped roof. The museum displays on three floors the history of the city through multimedia exhibits, photographs, old maps. For all the details see their website here http://ville.montreal.qc.ca/. South of the square, another building will attract your attention: **The House of Mother of Youville**. This building housed from 1695 to 1880 the old General Hospital of Montreal, built outside the fortifications to provide care to the poor. The architecture, very utilitarian, is rudimentary and was used for the constructions of religious communities. This art was transmitted from father to son since French Canadians had no architect at that time, due to the social rank of the colony. Another spot full of charm near the previous is the **Great Peace of Montreal Square**: that is a green area, between **Pointe-à-Callière**, Archelogy and History Museum of Montreal and the **Montreal history Center**. There are several commemorative plaques, an obelisk, the first well of the island of Montreal and a work of art of Gilles Mihalcean, entitled "The Fear". It consists of several elements: a cross, a disk, a stone, a bent finger.

Photo 11.13: Montreal History Center

If you have more days to spend in town, go strolling in St. Antoine Street (one-way if you are driving). At number 700 in the east portion of the street you'll find a beautiful train station: **La Gare Viger**. Commissioned in 1897, the monumental building looks like a castle, in eclectic style, and became a hotel in 1910. Another picturesque street is St. Hubert Street, oriented north-south and crosses the entire island of Montreal.

Photo 11.16: Botanical garden of Montreal

North of the Old Port, less than ten kilometers, you'll find the **Montreal Botanical Garden**. An oasis of 75 hectares where you can enjoy a long walk among the thirty thematic gardens (Chinese, aquatic, alpine, Japanese Gardens, etc.), marvel in the ten exhibition greenhouses, discover the Insectarium with over 200,000 specimens of mounted or living insects or the Planetarium. For all the details on the spaces, exhibitions, gardens, schedules and prices, see the website http://espacepourlavie.ca/en/. To benefit from attractive packages, see their website.

Photo 11.17: Botanical garden of Montreal

Photo 11.20: Olympic Stadium

Not far from the Botanical Garden, the Biodôme is really worth a visit. It's a "living" museum located in the former Velodrome of Montreal that was built for the Summer Olympics of 1976. The interior space of the building presents four of the ecosystems of the Americas: the Tropical Forest, the Laurentian Forest, the Gulf of Saint Lawrence and the Poles. Natural conditions such as temperature or humidity have been restored thanks to an ingenious system and relaxation areas have been created to allow visitors to admire the animals while resting.

Photo 11.21: The biosphere

If you still want to visit museums, go to St. Helena island, by subway, to see the Biosphere, dedicated to ecology and then the Fort Stewart with beautiful exhibitions. We visited them with the Museums Pass that we bought. There are also picnic areas and playgrounds for children.

A charming street with small restaurants, terraces and bars is *Rue Saint Denis*. Full of life at any hour of the day, it will make you travel because there are Japanese, Thai, Mexican restaurants.

We chose to stay near the airport in Montreal for several reasons: first the price, incomparable with those of city accommodation. Another reason was the free shuttle to the airport that makes life easier when arriving. You can buy tickets for all public transport to the airport distributors. There are several formulas. Be aware that the buses follow schedules registered at the bus shelter. If you think it is a solution for your needs, then I advise you DAYS INN Montreal Airport or the Travelodge nearby. We paid 673 CAD for 6 nights for 3 people... However, don't count on their pool or on the breakfast which is not included in the price!

12. Saint-Eustache

Saint-Eustache is a town from Quebec about twenty kilometers northwest of Montreal, at the mouth of the Chêne River and along the Two Mountains' Lake. It is a small town with few tourist attractions that are worth visiting if you have time.

In the city center there is the church of Saint-Eustache which has great historical significance for the city. Indeed, it had a key role in the Battle of Saint-Eustache during the 1837 rebellion. The church was ravaged by a violent fire sparked by British troops to expel the Patriots who had found refuge inside. The reconstruction lasted several years.

Photo 12.2: Art Center of the small church

Photo 12.3: Mansion Globensky

Not far from the church you can find another one, built in 1910 to replace the one that was destroyed in a fire. Today this charming little church houses the "Art Center of the small church" that hosts shows, concerts and plays. If you want to see the program, go to their website here https://www.lapetiteeglise.com/. For art lovers, there is the mansion Globensky, a bourgeois house with Victorian and Néo-Georgian influences, which now houses the "House of Culture and Heritage" with several exhibitions on the history of the city. Another visit in this small town can be done at the watermill Légaré, the oldest still in use in Canada. It produces dozens of tons of flour per year, while respecting the traditional production methods. For other ideas of visit see the website here http://www.vieuxsainteustache.com/

13. Laval

Laval is a great city of Quebec about twenty kilometers north of Montreal, located on Jésus Island, and bordered by two rivers: Thousand Islands and Prairies' Rivers. If you are in Montreal, you can go to Laval by subway.

Photo 13.1: Boulevard des Mille-Iles

If you have time to take a walk in the city, do it on the Thousand Islands Boulevard that goes along the river of the same name, because you'll discover plenty of nice houses in different styles, wood or brick, with charming little gardens.

If you like the shows and music, go to the House of Arts that presents a selection of the best performances of theater and dance, as well as exhibitions of visual arts at the Alfred-Pellan room. For the program and other details, see here http://www.laval.ca/maisondesarts/.

A must visit in Laval is the Nature Centre, a park spread over 50 hectares and where young and old will find plenty of activities: kayaking on the lake, hiking on 5 km of flowered or wooded trails, even skiing or ice skating during the winter. For the children there are several playgrounds, a tropical greenhouse to explore, and a farm to discover. For all the activities see the city website.

In Sainte-Rose Boulevard, there is the former convent of the Sisters of Holy Cross, built in 1876 in Neo-classical style, with Second European Empire influences, very fashionable at that time. Under the bell-cast roof there is a beautiful woodwork with Greek dentil cornice and on the main facade there are three Palladian style windows.

If you travel with children or are passionate about space, there is a museum not to miss in Laval: the Cosmodôme. It offers exhibitions and educational activities related to space and space exploration. The Space Camp allows visitors to learn the training of real astronauts, by trying simulators like those of NASA: weightlessness, disorientation and other sensations are scheduled. There is a circuit of six rooms composed of films and games where the visitor can perform three space missions: the impossible dream, the red planet or to the borders of the cosmos. For all the details on the exhibits, schedules and prices see their website here https://www.cosmodome.org/en/.

14. Gatineau

Gatineau is a city of Quebec, along the Ottawa River, 200 km west of Montreal and less than 10 km from Ottawa, Canada's capital. It forms with the latter the metropolitan area of Ottawa-Gatineau (National Capital Region), which is the fourth urban area of the country, after Toronto, Montreal and Vancouver. The city has some tourist attractions.

 The most visited attraction in Gatineau is

probably the Canadian Museum of History that houses permanent exhibitions covering 20,000 years of human history of Canada. It is located on the banks of the river and easily recognizable by its modern architecture. For information on exhibits, schedules and prices, visit their website. It also shelters another museum that will delight children: The Canadian Children's Museum. Its permanent exhibition is called "The Great Adventure" and consists in an interactive and intercultural travel: with a passport issued by the museum and a lot of imagination, the travelers can visit Japan, India, Mexico and Indonesia, among other international destinations. For all the details on the activities and schedules see their website here https://www.historymuseum.ca/visit/childrens-museum/.

Photo 14.2: Gatineau Park - Pink Lake

Another visit you should do in the area is the Gatineau Park. With several hundreds of hectares, it is located west of the Gatineau River and is full of attractions for those who love nature and outdoor activities. There are over 150 km of hiking trails for all levels and 90 km of mountain bike trails. The easiest and the shortest trail is that of Lac-des-Fées and runs along the lake for one kilometer. An ideal place for birdwatching is located at the southern end of the park near Gatineau's city center. Another trail is the one at the edge of Pink Lake, a lake with turquoise water surrounded by forests that I highly recommend. You can even see small turtles at the edge of the lake. Another trail that is worth it is that of King Mountain, on almost 2 km, leading to the Eardley Escarpment forming the boundary between the Canadian Shield and the St. Lawrence Lowlands. It rises 300 meters above the Ottawa Valley. This escarpment benefits from a warm and dry microclimate, being home to many rare species of plants and animals. If you are lucky and patient, you may be able to spot a white-tailed deer, a Canadian beaver, a groundhog, or a gray squirrel. There are also many birds to watch at the edge of the park's lakes: herons, Canada geese (those black and white headed and black necked geese), full of species of ducks, American kingfishers, picks, etc. The **Transcanadian trail** passes through the park and is the longest network of recreational trails in the world! If you want to rent a kayak, a paddle boat or a canoe, you can do it at Philippe Lake or Fishing Lake. For prices and details see here. For details on summer or winter activities, accommodation, prices see the park's website.

Photo 14.4: Gatineau Park - hike of Eardley Escarpment

If you like playing at the casino, there is one in Gatineau: the complex of the Casino of Lac-Leamy, with a 5 star hotel - if you have the means to pay a room there or if you won at the roulette! - and several restaurants. For information see their website https://casinos.lotoquebec.com/en/portal/home.

If you like train trips or if you travel with children, then go for a trip with the steam train of Hull-Chelsea-Wakefield which runs, from May to October, on 64 km between Gatineau and the tourist village of Wakefield. It starts from the station located at 165 Devault Street and crosses the municipality of Chelsea. At its destination, a manual turntable, one of the few still operating in Canada, allows the turn of the device 180 degrees to return to Hull. The journey takes an hour and a half and allows you appreciate the landscapes over hills and the Gatineau River.

15. Percé

Percé is a village from Quebec, located at the head of the Gaspé Peninsula in front of the famous rock of the same name and Bonaventure Island, 760 km southwest of Quebec.

Even if Percé is almost at the end of the world, the beauty of its landscapes is well known and is worth the trip. The village covers about three kilometers between the peak of Dawn and the Surprise Coast. The Percé Rock, dug by natural arches, is 86 meters high and serves as a den for gannets, those birds with white feathers, head and yellow pale neck and black tipped wings. At low tide it's possible to reach the rock on foot, on a pebble path. The natural amphitheater of Percé is dominated by Mount Sainte-Anne and Mont Blanc, which rises to over 350 meters and with slopes mostly covered by forests.

Photo 15.1: Percé and its rock

Another must visit in the area is the National Park of Bonaventure and Percé Rock Island that includes the famous rock and Bonaventure Island, home to the largest colony of gannets in the world. It is a small park with an area of less than 6 km², but you can see animals such as the red fox, stoat or snowshoe hare. In the waters of the park you can see - if you are lucky - seals, porpoises, dolphins or rorquals.

The village's beautiful church attracts attention with its small white turrets contrasting with the brown stone of the building.

If you want to find accommodation in Percé, see this website https://www.tourisme-gaspesie.com/en/decouvrir/regions/la-pointe.html where there is also plenty of information about the activities and tourist attractions of the area.

There are several sandy beaches in the region: that of the Anse-à-Beaufils, Coin-du-Banc where there is also a charming little village to discover, or a little further to the south, the Anse Carnival up to the Newport area.

Canada: general presentation of the country

Canada is a country in North America, the second largest in the world after Russia. With its 35 million inhabitants, Canada is a federal constitutional monarchy with a parliamentary system consisting of ten provinces and three territories. Provinces:

1. Alberta

2. British Colombia

3. Prince Edward Island

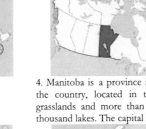

4. Manitoba is a province in the west of the country, located in the region of grasslands and more than one hundred thousand lakes. The capital is Winnipeg.

5. New Brunswick is a province southeast of the country where a third of the population is French-speaking. Its capital is Fredericton.

6. Nova Scotia is a province on the Atlantic coast with the capital in Halifax.

7. Ontario is located next to the province of Quebec and has more than 13 million inhabitants. It is located in the east central part of the country. Its capital is Toronto, the largest city of the country. On its territory there is also Ottawa, the federal capital of Canada. We traveled through this province during our trip and were impressed by the Niagara Falls, but also by the bogs, landscapes and lakes throughout the province.

8. Quebec is a province in the east, with its capital having the same name. It is a gorgeous region that you will find described in this eGuide because we had the chance to visit it. Crossed by the St. Lawrence River, Quebec has a population of eight million people, mainly composed of Francophones. It is the only province that has as official language French.

9. Saskatchewan is a western province of Canada, located in the prairie region and its capital is in Regina.

10. Newfoundland and Labrador is an eastern province of Canada, located in the Atlantic region. The majority of its population lives on the island of Newfoundland. Its capital is St. John's.

Capital: **Ottawa** is the federal capital of Canada. It was founded in 1826 during the construction of the Rideau Canal and was first called Bytown. It houses the government institutions of the country, such as the Parliament, the residences of the General Governor and the Prime Minister. The name of the city comes from the Ottawa River that borders it and it has nearly 900,000 inhabitants.

Geography: Surface: approx.. 10 million km²

Population: 35.7 million inhabitants.

Spoken languages: The official languages are English and French.

Currency: The national currency is the Canadian dollar.

Infrastructure: Canada has a vast road network, which allows you to drive between the most remote destinations. The roads are mostly in good condition, even though the consequences of winter weather are visible on some of them. The railway network crosses the country from Halifax, in Nova Scotia, to the east, up to Vancouver and Prince Rupert, in British Columbia, to the west. The trains are comfortable. For information or to purchase tickets go see Via Rail Canada's website. Another means of transport in coastal regions of Canada such as British Columbia and the Atlantic region, but also on the rivers as in Quebec is the ferry. Many ferries carry both passengers and vehicles.

Climate: There are seven types of climate in Canada. Most of the country has a sub-Arctic climate that extends into the southern part of the Northwest Territories and Nunavut, in north-eastern British Columbia, northern Prairies, from Ontario and Quebec up to Labrador. In the north of the Yukon, Northwest Territories and Nunavut there is an Arctic climate. A dry continental climate is in the southern Prairies. In the provinces of Quebec, Ontario and northwestern New Brunswick there is a wet continental climate. A Marine climate is in the area of the Pacific coast of British Columbia, but also in the Atlantic Provinces (New Brunswick, Prince Edward Island, Nova Scotia and island of Newfoundland). An Alpine climate characterizes most of British Columbia, Yukon and southwestern Alberta. Winter can be very severe in some parts of the country, with average monthly temperatures that can go down to -15°C in the south and even -45°C in the north. The annual snowfall can reach

several hundred centimeters on average. The coast of British Columbia, including Vancouver Island, is an exception, with a Temperate climate with mild, rainy winters. In summer temperatures can climb to 35°C, even 40°C. For the weather forecast for Canada, there is this government site https://weather.gc.ca/canada_e.html which is very complete.

History: Some regions of Canada were inhabited by Amerindian and Inuit peoples for thousands of years. These indigenous people have arrived in America through their migration by the Isthmus of Beringia between Alaska and eastern Siberia. The first European explorations began on the coasts of Labrador and the island of Newfoundland, which were visited by the Vikings, Normans and probably the Basques since the first millennium. The Venetian explorers Giovanni Caboto and his son Sebastian landed in Bonavista (Newfoundland) in 1497 on behalf of King Henry VII of England. The Portuguese João Fernandes Lavrador explored around 1500 the Labrador's current coast that bears his name. The French explorer Jacques Cartier visited Newfoundland, the Gulf of St. Lawrence, the Magdalen Islands and Prince Edward Island. Then finally, in 1534 he landed in Gaspé where he took possession of the land in the name of the king of France, Francis the Ist. A French colony was founded along the banks of the St. Lawrence River. Tadoussac built in 1600 the first permanent French fort, origin of the present village of the same name at the mouth of the Saguenay River. Between 1598 and 1603, Henri IV charged Troilus de La Roche de Mesgouez, as lieutenant general of the countries of Canada, Newfoundland, Labrador and Norembègue, to establish a new post of colonization in New France. This second attempt at colonization occurred on Sable Island, located off the current Nova Scotia. King Louis XIII placed the governor of New France directly under the authority of Cardinal Richelieu since he had become chief minister of the state in 1624 until his death in 1642. In 1627 is created the seigneurial system, the main mode of administration of lands of New France. At the first conquest of 1629, New France passed under British rule when the merchant Sir David Kirke took possession of the fort and the Château Saint-Louis after the assault on the city of Quebec where he forced Samuel de Champlain to surrender, forcibly sent to Britain. England gave back New France to France in 1632 at the signing of the Treaty of Saint-Germain-en-Laye. On his return in 1633, Samuel de Champlain built the church Notre-Dame-de-Recouvrance thus naming to highlight the fact that France had regained its colony.

The competition for territories, naval bases, furs and fish became terrible, causing many wars between the French, the Dutch, the British and the Native American tribes as allies. Thus, the XVIIIth century is dominated by inter-colonial wars between the French, having as allies the Hurons and Algonquins, and the Dutch as well as the British later, which had as allies the Iroquois, in order to establish the control of the fur trade.

The governor Louis de Buade de Frontenac has built the first enclosure of the Citadel of Quebec in 1690 to protect the city.

After the British conquest in America and the end of the Seven Years

War in Europe, New France disappeared completely by remaining under British rule. By the Royal Proclamation made in 1763 under commission of King George III, Canada has changed its name by becoming the Province of Quebec. From 1763 to 1766, the Ottawa Indians rose against the British. The English then unleashed a biological war by distributing blankets infected with the smallpox virus in Indian forts. During the Battle of Quebec in 1775, the Americans attacked the British at Quebec to try to seize the city in order to lift the French Canadians against Great Britain and to win their support in the quest for independence of the United States. Despite this defeat, the city of Montreal and the Richelieu River forts were forced to surrender. A project of parliamentary constitution is established, and a legislative assembly is constituted in 1791. The province of Quebec is divided by the Constitutional Act of 1791 into two distinct colonies: Upper Canada and Lower Canada.

The Act of the British North America in 1867 has created a dominion under the name of Canada, with four distinct provinces: Ontario, Quebec, New Brunswick and Nova Scotia. The purpose of this organization was to drown the French-speaking Quebec, in a group of small English-speaking provinces with the same powers as well as to protect themselves against the expansionist ideas of the United States after the American Civil War. After a turbulent history during the two wars, a massive immigration from various states ravaged in Europe has changed the country's demographic curve. April the 17th, 1982, Canada repatriated its Constitution of Great Britain, under proclamation of Queen Elizabeth II. This act of the British Parliament created a fully sovereign state, although the two countries still share today the same monarch. With the Constitution Act of 1982, the state form of Canada changed from a confederation to a federation, giving way to a Canadian federalism. Since the late XIXth century Native Americans administer quasi-autonomous territories, called reserves, granted by the federal government. Indigenous peoples do not pay taxes neither provincial taxes. Canada is a constitutional monarchy that recognizes Queen Elizabeth II as Queen of Canada since her coronation on the 6th of February 1952. In his capacity as representative of the Queen, David Lloyd Johnston, General Governor since 2010, Chief Commander of the Canadian Forces assumes royal prerogatives when the Queen is not in Canada. He is appointed by the Queen on advice of the Prime Minister and his residence is Rideau Hall in Ottawa, as well as the Citadel of Quebec.

Useful links and information

History, geography: To know the history of this country see the Wikipedia page or this website. For the geography see here https://www.canadashistory.ca/.

General and practical information: A website with useful information for a traveler in Canada can be found here https://caen-keepexploring.canada.travel/ and another here http://www.vacancescanada.com/pratique/.

Tourism: A useful site for travelers http://caen-

keepexploring.canada.travel.

Car rentals: To have all the car rental companies at the Montreal Airport see here. We rented a car for 22 days for 965 € on this website http://www.rentalcars.com/ insurance included.

Credits

We thank Wikipedia and OpenStreetMap for the free resources used in the development of this guide (photographs, maps, etc.). We are grateful to all contributors to these sites without whom we would not be able to complete some of our articles. Also thanks to all the kind souls who offer online tools and free resources to use for those who still want to learn and improve!

Photo credits:

Photo 8.1: « Deschambault church 2 » par Harfang — Travail personnel. Sous licence CC BY 3.0 via Wikimedia Commons

Authors

Cristina and Olivier Rebière met at the age of 17 in 1990 in Romania, shortly after the fall of the Berlin Wall and the Romanian Revolution of December 1989. After two years of correspondence and several meetings, Cristina was able to get a scholarship to study in France and became Olivier's wife in 1993. Since then, these two "life adventurers" have had an existence full of twists and turns, during which they fell in love with travel, entrepreneurship and writing. Their books are useful, practical, and will fill you up with energy and creativity. Discover all the Cristina & Olivier's collections on the website http://www.OlivierRebiere.com

Made in United States
North Haven, CT
16 July 2022

21448746R00035